JE

Jaynes, Ruth

Tell me please! What's that?

TELL ME
PLEASE!
WHAT'S
THAT?

Library of Congress Catalog Card Number 68-17028
International Standard Book Number 0-8372-0267-1

1 2 3 4 5 6 7 8 9 84 83 82 81 80 79 78 77 76 75

Bowmar Early Childhood Series

TELL ME PLEASE! WHAT'S THAT?

written by Ruth Jaynes

photographed by Harvey Mandlin

Bowmar Publishing Corp.
Glendale, California

This is Juan.   This is David.   Juan and David are friends.   They have good times together.

Juan speaks Spanish. He wants to speak English.

David speaks English. He wants to speak Spanish.

One day David's mother took the boys to the Children's Zoo. Through the gate they went to see all the animals.

CHILDREN'S ZOO

AGE 6 AND OVER 15¢
AGE 5 AND UNDER FREE

Juan was excited!

He said, "Un pato! Es un pato!

Tell me, please! What's that?"

David said, "A duck! It's a duck!"
"Quack, quack," said the duck.

Juan saw a white furry animal.

"Un conejo," he said. "Es un conejo!

Tell me, please! What's that?"

David said, "A rabbit! It's a rabbit!"

Then David saw another animal.

"Tell me, please! What's that?" he asked.

Juan laughed. He said, "Un pollo! Es un pollo!
A chicken! It's a chicken!"
"Cluck, cluck," said the chicken.

All at once they heard, "Ma-a-a, ma-a-a."

"Un cabrito!   Es un cabrito," said Juan.

"Tell me, please! What's that?"

"A baby goat," said David. "It's a baby goat."

"Quack, quack," "Ma-a-a, ma-a-a."
The animals say it's time to be fed.
"Here is the man with their lunch," said David.

"Would you like to help?" asked the man.

"Oh, yes!" said David.

"Si!" said Juan.

At last David's mother said, "It's time to go."

"Adiós, animales," said Juan. "Adiós."

And David said, "Good-by, animals, good-by."

The End

PICTURE BOOKS IN THE BOWMAR EARLY CHILDHOOD SERIES

Part One:
ABOUT MYSELF

Do You Know What...?
Melissa Lou has begun to discover that she is a person of capability and worth, special and distinct from all others as she enjoys her own particular place with the members of her family, her teacher and classmates.

What Is A Birthday Child?
This book shows a little girl experiencing the most important event in a young child's life—her own day—her birthday. Through simple recognition of this day, Juanita, and other children, are helped to see themselves as unique persons, worthy of recognition and celebration.

Father Is Big
The father role is portrayed here in terms that are understandable to the child, through showing *bigness* and strength in exquisite photographs. Even for children from fatherless homes the book pictures an understandable family relationship, and holds hope for the child that he may one day become *big* and achieve his role as a strong family member.

The Littlest House
Living in a very small house, even a tiny mobile home, can be the source of many delightful experiences and lively conversations, as seen in this happy, personal *tour* of "The Littlest House."

The Biggest House
Houses differ, but they all shelter families, and this one shelters many! As one family, among many, living in "the biggest house on the street" Robert tells about all the things he can do, people he can know, and, most of all, about the pride he has in this special place—his home.

Friends! Friends! Friends!
Through the person-to-person relationships depicted in this book, the young child, like Kimi, becomes more aware of friendship experiences in his own classroom.

My Friend is Mrs. Jones
With his adult friend and neighbor a little boy enjoys helping, being helped, and doing things with this sensitive, older companion. Through this relationship children are helped to identify with this child, in verbalizing and in finding ways of their own to be friends.

Part Two:
THE WORLD AROUND ME

Let Me See You Try
Readiness to attempt new tasks of physical involvement are encouraged through the joyful participation of many children as they skip, clap, tiptoe and as they ask questions, such as, "Can you skip in a circle?" and add, "Let me see you try!"

My Tricycle and I
A tricycle ride with the little boy in the story encourages children to develop a greater awareness of many basic physical and sensory learnings. At the same time the imaginative delights of a *pretend* ride, at the child's level of pretence, is explored.

Watch Me Outdoors
Children in the sand box, sharing Denny's experiences, will become more aware of the sensory and imaginative uses of sand and water. They will be involved in the best of learning situations for the young child, *play*.

Watch Me Indoors
The enthusiasm of a little girl showing her special visitor—her mother—all the things she can do at school will help children everywhere to identify with and enjoy more their expanding store of accomplishments.

Follow The Leader
As the children in this story enthusiastically participate in important motor development, they gradually learn how to use and control their bodies, at the same time reinforcing the language development that so often accompanies this type of learning through play.

Melinda's Christmas Stocking
Melinda's immediate world takes on new meaning as she sees, touches, smells, hears and tastes the various objects she finds in her Christmas stocking.

Listen!
An introduction to some of the sounds commonly heard in the places children commonly go — the park, the city, school and home. Greater interest in and sensitivity to these and other sounds in our environment is encouraged through the delightful presentation in this basic book of sounds.

A Box Tied with a Red Ribbon
All the children try to guess what is in the box that Nancy brings to school. "Is it a toy?" "Can we play with it?" They shake the box. They open it. The surprise box excites all five senses as the children explore all the possibilities of its contents.

An Apple is Red
How does an apple look when you bite it? When you dry a grape, does it still look like a grape? Keener observation of shape, color and taste are invited and encouraged through the esthetic presentation of beginning science concepts.

Part Three:
I TALK—I THINK—I REASON

What Do You Say?
Many ways of saying the same thing are introduced through the visit of two children and a friendly adult to a supermarket carnival. The child hears his own vocabulary used and at the same time is introduced to new expressions equally usable.

Furry Boy
As the children take care of a pet rabbit this stimulating environment brings about much real language development. Their love and growing reliability as they care for Furry Boy is also apparent in every word and picture.

Tell Me, Please! What's That?
David speaks English. Juan speaks Spanish. The different kinds of animals in the Children's Zoo motivate David and Juan to talk, and the vocabulary of each is expanded as the boys understand and use the other's language.

Funny Mr. Clown
While increasing their capacity for humor through real experiences and the preposterous statement, the children are finding joy in seeing a clown do tricks for their own class.

Benny's Four Hats
Observations and comparisons by children are always necessary in the building of ideas and growth in ability to reason. As Benny puts on, and wears each of his hats, children will use these meaningful tools in *guessing* why Benny wears each hat, and then *seeing* why he did in the story.

Where Is Whiffen?
Both reasoning and persistence are demonstrated at a child's level of understanding as Jimmy tries to find his dog, Whiffen. After several unsuccessful attempts to find Whiffen, Jimmy arrives at a successful solution.

That's What It Is!
A lively curiosity is the basis for the desire to learn, and in this book, Marcus' actions show that his curiosity has been encouraged. Children, as they enjoy Marcus' adventure will become more curious, themselves, will want to explore, to investigate, to question.

Do You Suppose Miss Riley Knows?
On his most important day, his birthday, Rudy wonders if his teacher will remember. Gradually, through all the special occurrences, he reasons that she *must* know and finally that she *does* know.

A Beautiful Day For a Picnic
A beautiful day, a packed lunch, a long, long walk, play in the sunshine, eating lunch outdoors—these are a picnic! The formation of a concept begins to occur, when with adult help children begin to relate information around a core idea.

Colors
Although children grow up in a world surrounded by color, too many live from day to day totally unaware of its beauty, variety and excitement. The book, "Colors", presents all three of these elements—beauty, variety and excitement—in such a way as to inspire maximum carryover into the live world of color around us.

Three Baby Chicks
Three children show their fascination with the ending of a long classroom vigil—the hatching of three baby chicks! To the very young child whose world must often seem to be made of magic the unfolding of events such as this begin to help him reason, to interpret and to understand how and why things happen.

I Like Cats
The concepts that begin to form in a child's mind about the variety of behavior of similar animals is strengthened as the little girl in this story shows her obvious pleasure in cats, and particularly in *her* cat.

Morning
What does *morning* mean to a child? Out of the thousands of early-in-the-day experiences every child has, some have come to mean morning. This story sorts out some of these commonly shared experiences and helps children to a greater awareness of morning.

Evening
What makes *evening?* The routine things that families do at this time of the day are delightfully pictured in this book where every page expresses the love and security that all children need.

Bowmar Publishing Corp.
Glendale, California